TOBINISMS

A handbook of inspiring and practical
leadership quotes and stories

By Peg Tobin, R.N.

Copyright © 2019 by Peg Tobin

Printed in the United States of America

First Edition, 2019

ISBN: 9781708468156

Contact Information:

Peg Tobin

8233 Howe Industrial Parkway

Canal Winchester, OH 43110

www.tobinway.com

ACKNOWLEDGEMENTS

To God for gifting me with enthusiasm and confidence to go where I am afraid. Thank you for the ability to visualize my dreams and thoughts.

To my fantastic husband, Richard, you have been by my side for every dream. Without your support this book would have never come to fruition. I am a very blessed woman to have you in my life.

To William (Marty, my oldest son), you have been my rock throughout this book adventure. You have held the business together while your mom went off and dreamed again. Thank you son, you make me so very proud and you help make all my dreams come true.

To Christopher (Chris, my youngest son), you approve me and encourage me. If only I could see myself as your eyes see me. Thank you son, you delight my soul and your confidence in me helped me write this book. You let me dream and for that I am blessed.

To Darrell Donalds, you rock! Thank you for your humor and commitment, Without your artistic gifts this book would have not come to life. 'IT' really does mean 'I Teach' to you! I have learned so much from your wisdom and insight.

To Jami, thank you for walking in our company's doors in 2011. You have shown me what courage looks like and I am proud to call you friend. You have made an imprint in our company and in my life.

To Lisa, you joined me on this journey in 2010 and you have never blinked twice about your decision. Loyalty is your middle name and accountability is your drive. Thank you for your dedication and friendship.

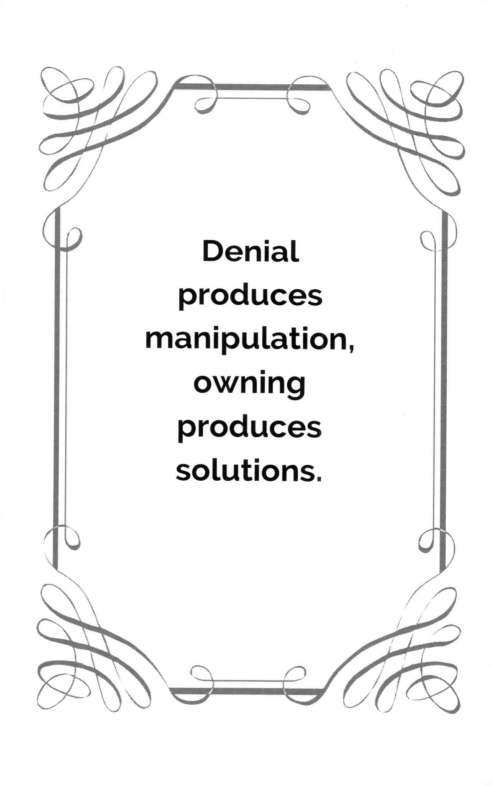

Denial
produces
manipulation,
owning
produces
solutions.

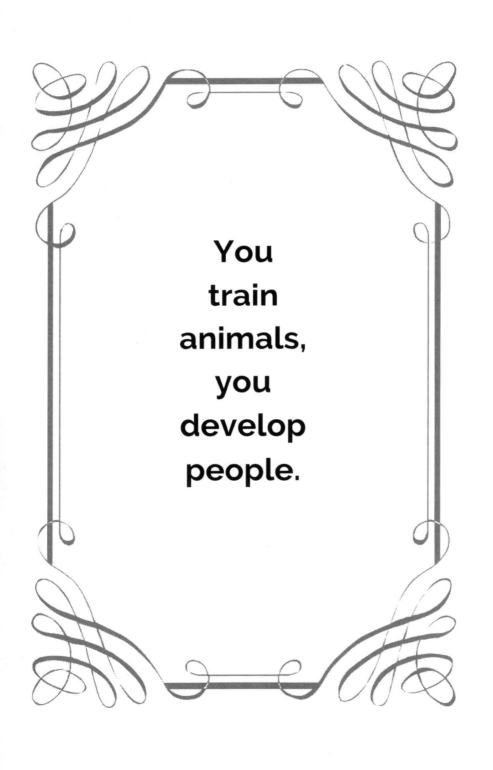

You
train
animals,
you
develop
people.

The power
within
is
the power
that wins.

When you
look at a raccoon
and you see a cat,
then to you
it is a cat!
This is called
personal
'perception'.

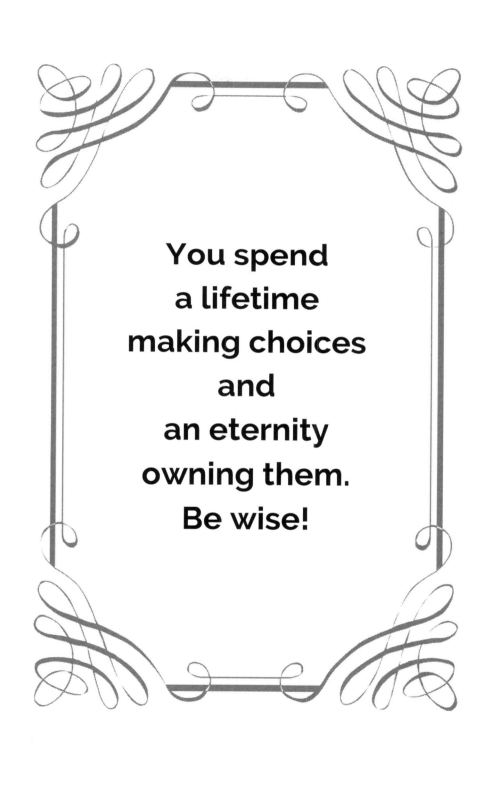

You spend
a lifetime
making choices
and
an eternity
owning them.
Be wise!

An open door
is an
opportunity.
Beyond the
threshold
is up to you!

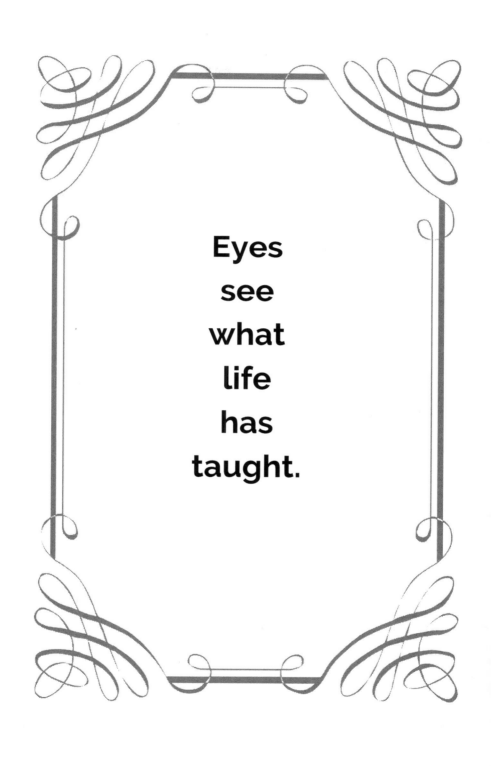

**Eyes
see
what
life
has
taught.**

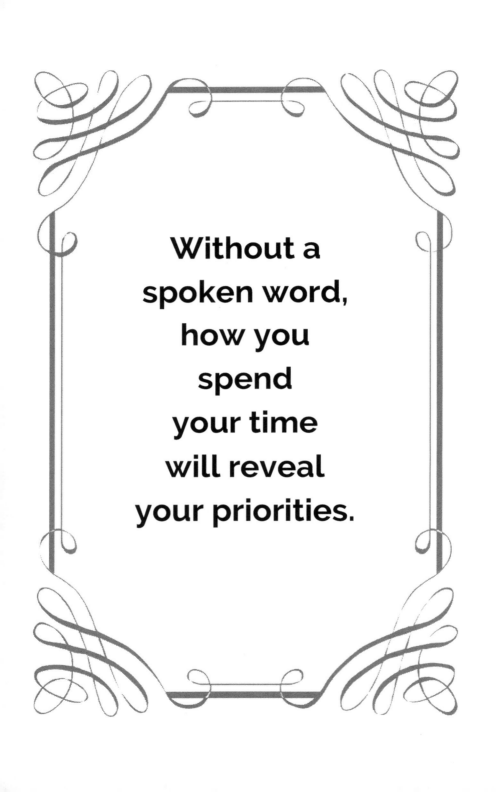

Without a
spoken word,
how you
spend
your time
will reveal
your priorities.

Buying material before you can visualize your product, is like spending money for oceanfront property in a dessert.

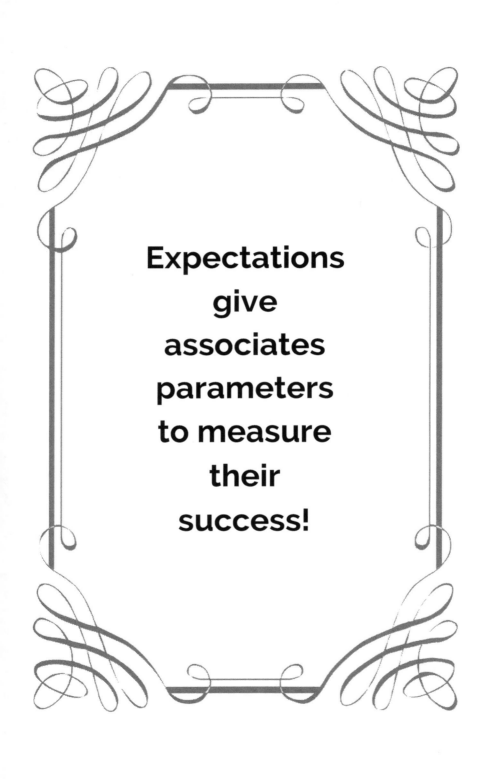

Expectations give associates parameters to measure their success!

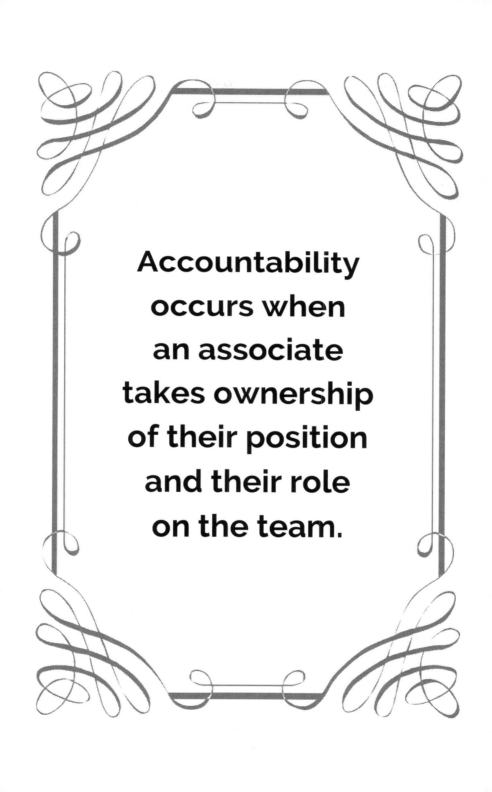

Accountability occurs when an associate takes ownership of their position and their role on the team.

Successful Leaders:

- are transparent
- are honest
- are humble
- know when to admit they are wrong

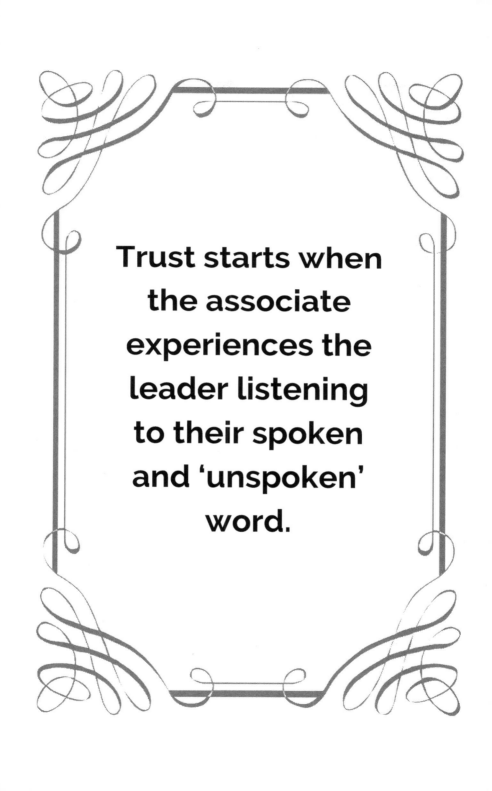

Trust starts when the associate experiences the leader listening to their spoken and 'unspoken' word.

**Sometimes
it takes
20 years
to be
discovered
overnight.**

The only
alternative
to
growing old
is
dying!

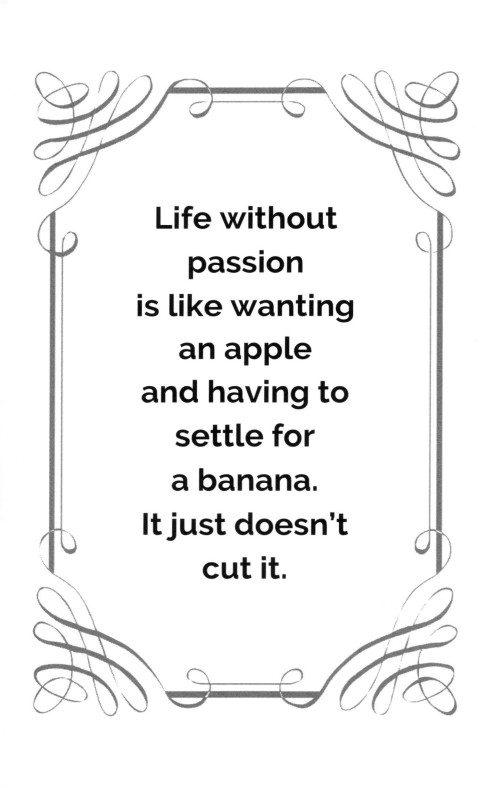

Life without
passion
is like wanting
an apple
and having to
settle for
a banana.
It just doesn't
cut it.

The best gifts
are lessons
that change
your life
for the better!

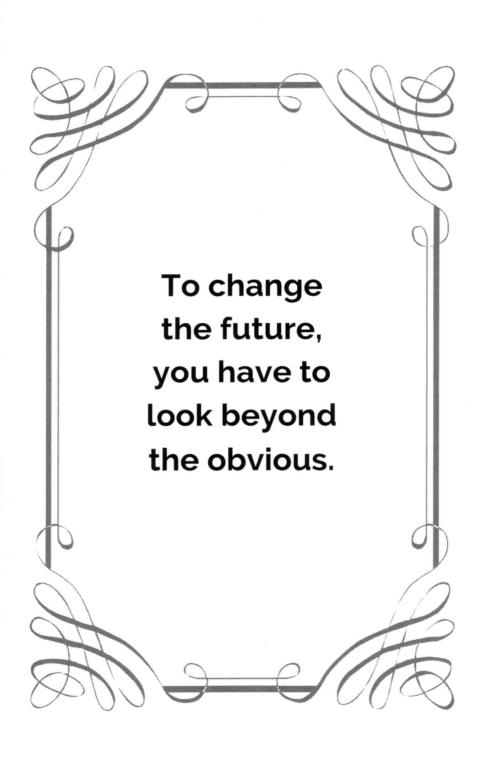

To change
the future,
you have to
look beyond
the obvious.

Seeing the world through another's eyes starts with closing your own eyes.

Lead with compassion. Hire with wisdom. Promote with humility.

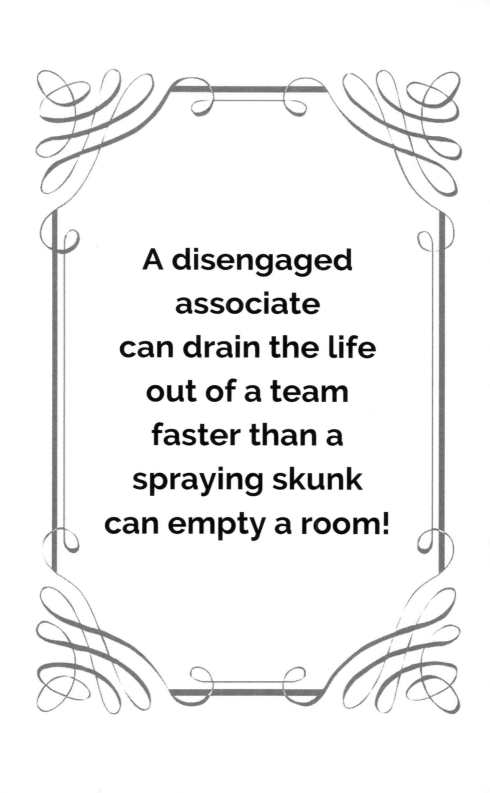

A disengaged
associate
can drain the life
out of a team
faster than a
spraying skunk
can empty a room!

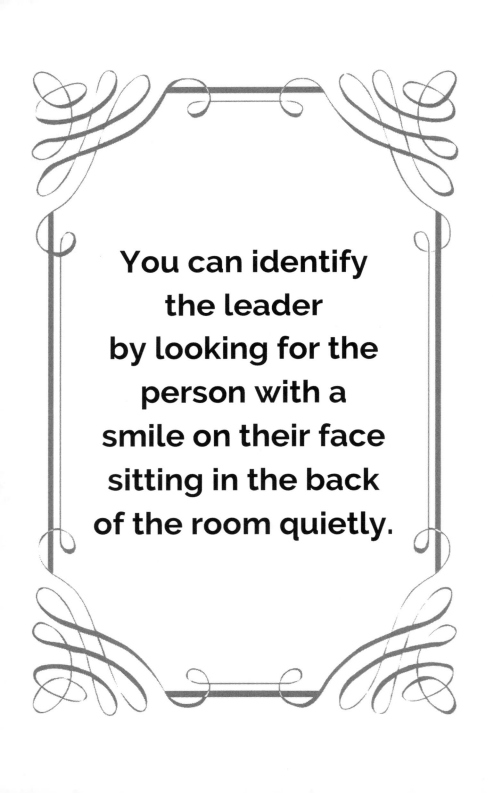

You can identify
the leader
by looking for the
person with a
smile on their face
sitting in the back
of the room quietly.

Misfortune offers
two choices:

Wallow in misery and
become the victim.
or
Learn and move
on to victory.

Successful Leaders start with 'top of mind' to make a difference. Money is just a by-product of their passion!

Leadership - On Air

The other day I leaned over, pushed a button to turn the TV on. There was a commentator speaking about how we in America are puppets and we can be swayed to make a decision and pushed in any direction with enough media coverage, blah, blah, blah......in a very short period of time I found this commentator was right; I was swayed by him. The decision I came to was this commentator was obnoxious and the direction I took was to change the station. With very little effort, I was able to push a button and like magic, the irritating chatter was over and out of my life.

As I pulled my hand back from the button on the TV, I wondered what if I came with a button like a TV and I was a show on leadership:

- Would I rank high in the Nielson ratings?
- Would people rush home to watch my leadership show?
- Would I be in focus – clear – understandable?
- Would I be a steady picture or flickering in and out?
- Would my picture fill the screen or have darkened parameters?
- Would I be up to date digital and have surround sound?
- Would my associates put a block on my show?
- Would I be a mystery, a soap opera, a success story, a documentary, a musical, a comedy, a satire or a science fiction?

- Would my show be like a variety show trying to entertain the masses?
- Would people want to tell others about my leadership show?

Or would people reach over, push my button and turn me off?

How about you, what kind of leadership show would you make?

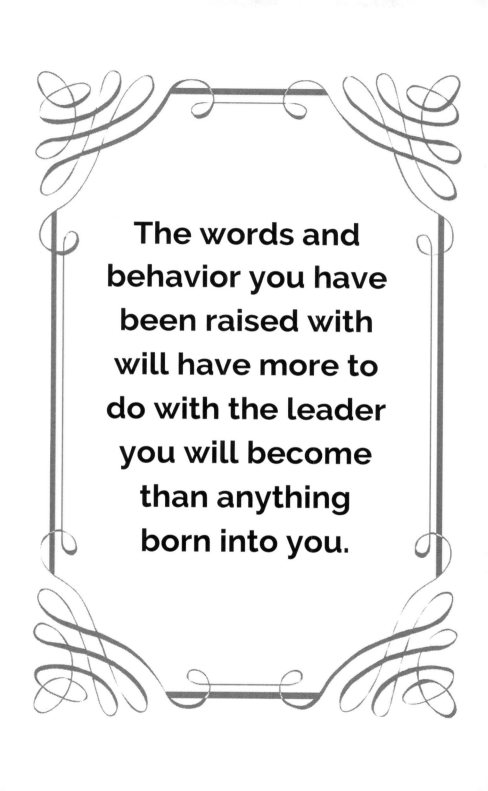

The words and behavior you have been raised with will have more to do with the leader you will become than anything born into you.

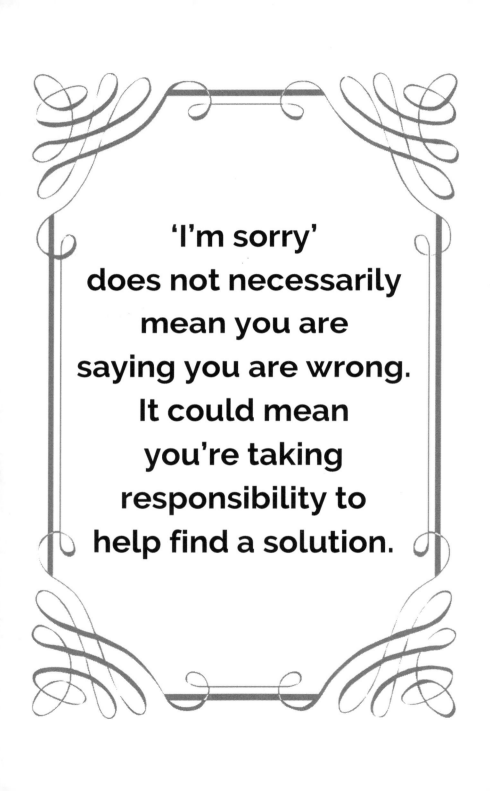

'I'm sorry'
does not necessarily
mean you are
saying you are wrong.
It could mean
you're taking
responsibility to
help find a solution.

You
get
what
you
expect.

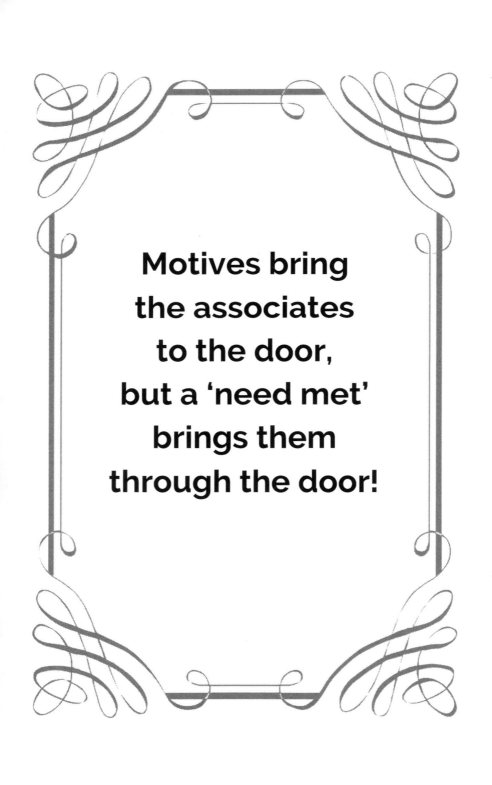

Motives bring
the associates
to the door,
but a 'need met'
brings them
through the door!

Build your
foundation
on truth and
honest practices,
and your company
will bear fruit
that will become
a lasting legacy.

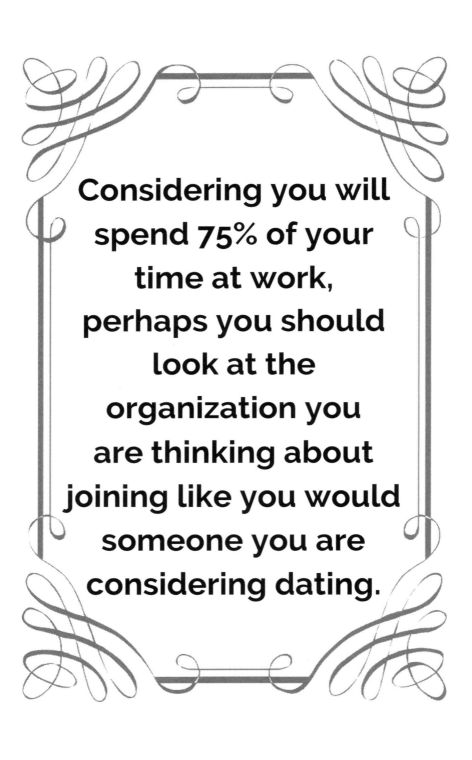

Considering you will spend 75% of your time at work, perhaps you should look at the organization you are thinking about joining like you would someone you are considering dating.

Solid Companies have:

- foundations built on integrity
- proven and caring leaders
- open communication
- passion for their product/services
- vision that goes beyond the present
- respect for all

Leadership
'sand traps' to avoid:

- being too nice
- not delegating/ empowering
- excessive paperwork
- inaccessibility
- pride (full of self)

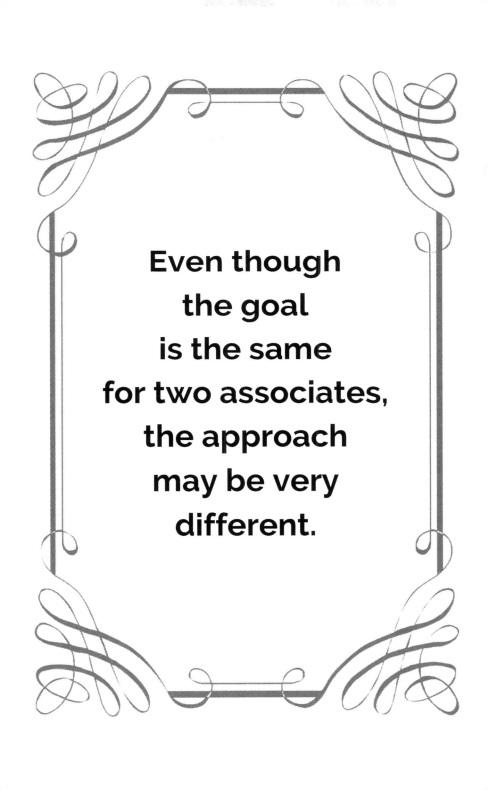

Even though
the goal
is the same
for two associates,
the approach
may be very
different.

When confronted with a challenge, leaders ask themselves:

- what part of this situation do I own?
- what can be changed?
- what cannot be changed?

A non-producing department can be much like junior high school:

- clicks
- bullies
- self-indulgence
- pointless behavior

Challenges
usually come
wrapped in fear.
However, fear
is nothing but
a state of mind
produced by
a lack of
knowledge.

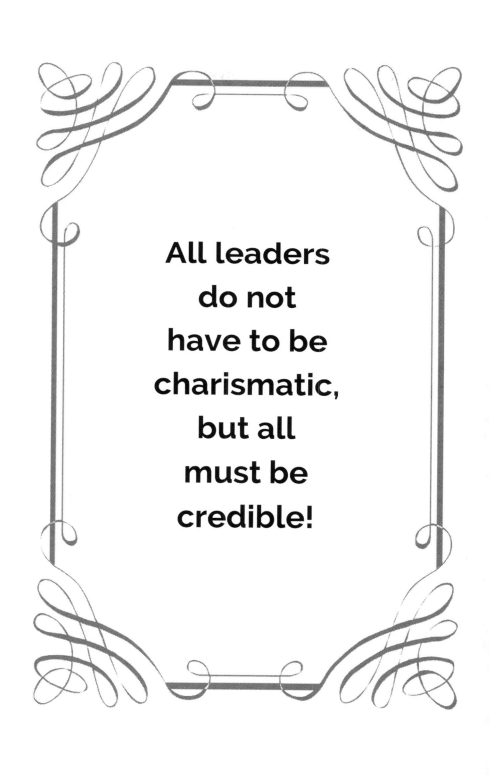

All leaders
do not
have to be
charismatic,
but all
must be
credible!

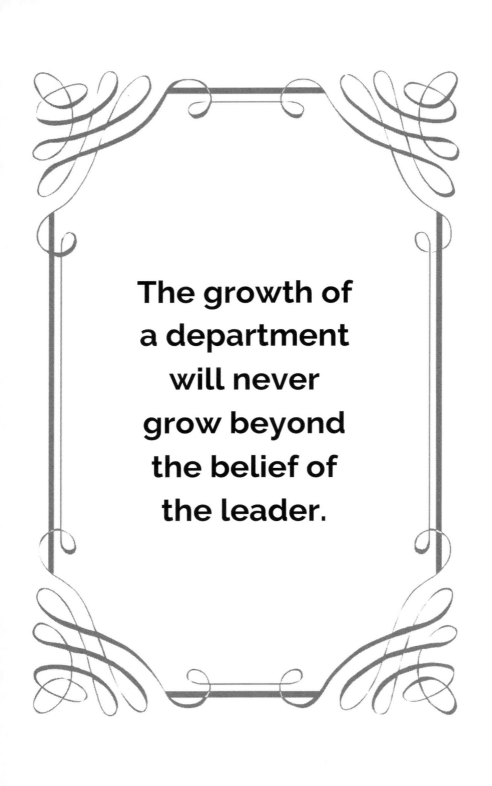

The growth of
a department
will never
grow beyond
the belief of
the leader.

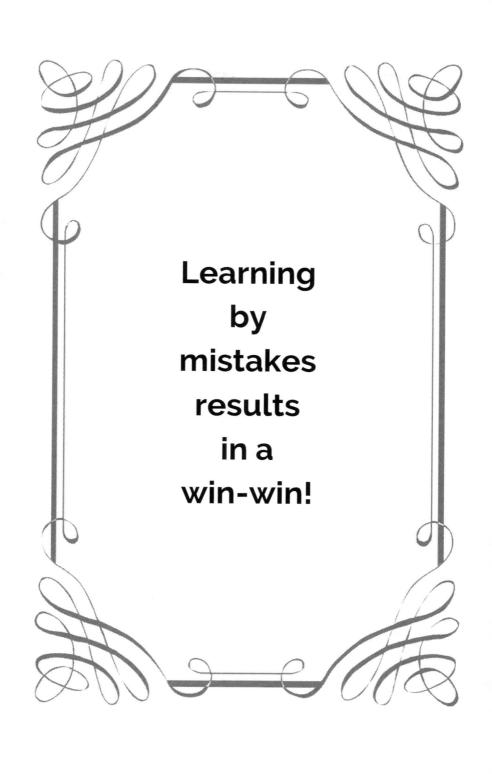

Learning
by
mistakes
results
in a
win-win!

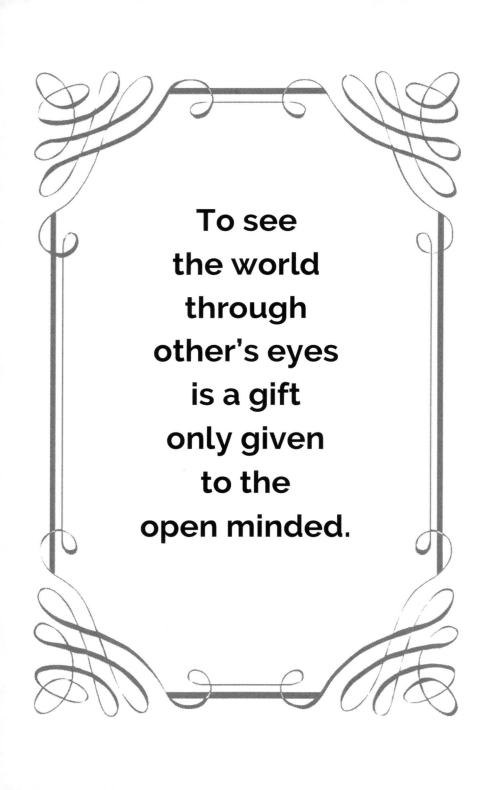

To see
the world
through
other's eyes
is a gift
only given
to the
open minded.

The longer
a leader waits
to get involved
with a disgruntled
associate, the
more entangled
the issues become.

If you hear a
'buzz'
long enough,
you know a
'sting'
is not far
behind!

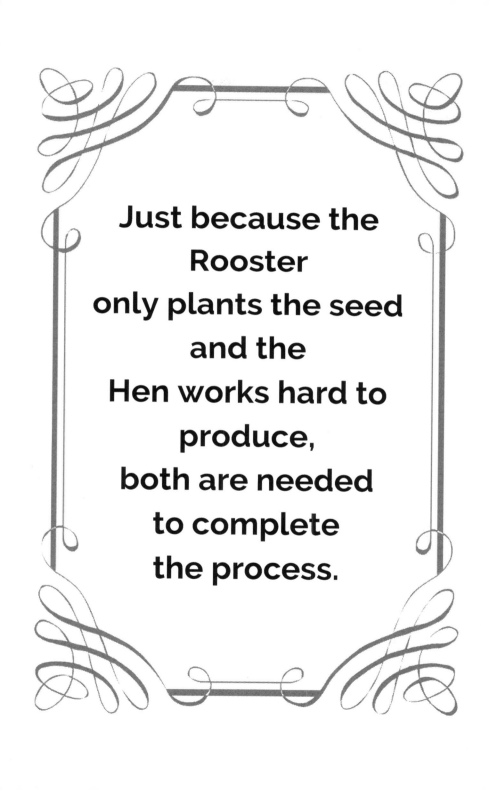

Just because the
Rooster
only plants the seed
and the
Hen works hard to
produce,
both are needed
to complete
the process.

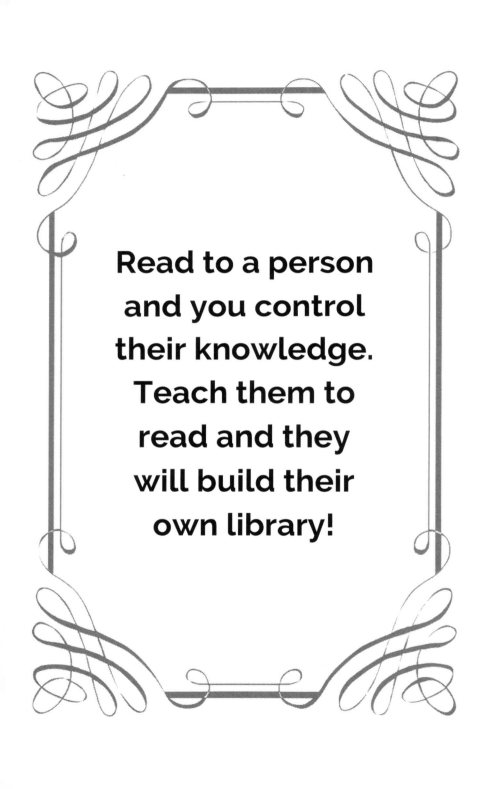

Read to a person and you control their knowledge. Teach them to read and they will build their own library!

Two actions that retain associates:

- respect
- recognition

Compliments
pave a
tough road
with hope!

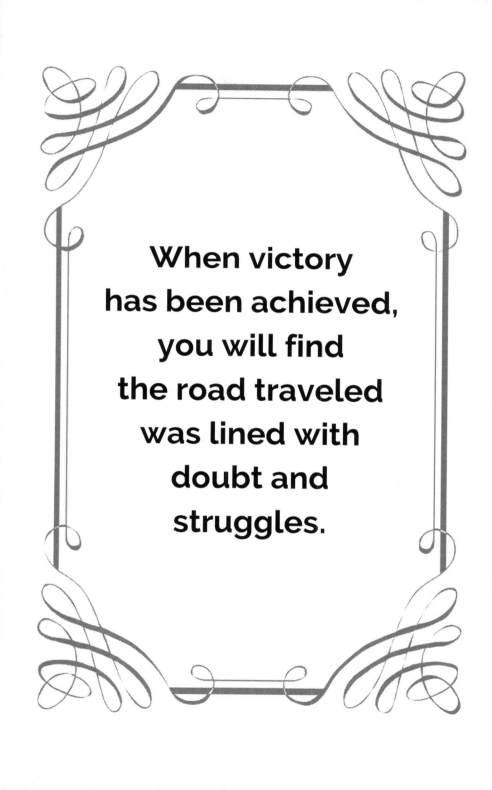

When victory
has been achieved,
you will find
the road traveled
was lined with
doubt and
struggles.

Stand tall
but do not overshadow.

Stand firm
but be not rigid.

Stand Consistent
but not unyielding.

Alligator Arms

"Wisdom takes root when you learn the best answer can be silence"

Choices are put in front of us every day as leaders. Not everything that happens to us is positive but the good news is we always have a choice on how we react. There are several paths to travel as a leader! Let's discuss two paths...

One path is that of the 'alligator arms' leader, it is safe and many travel it. It is said that the alligator arms leaders operates in:

"A state in which an individual does not travel nor reach outside of their comfort zone; therefore, they stay within what they view as safe and secure!"

- They protect their money by rarely reaching for the check at lunch meetings

- They avoid deep conversations

- They live by their title

- They avoid risks

- They do things that are beneficial and safe for them

- They remain with an organization as long as the organization is strong

- They allow others to take blame

- They redirect questions to others

- They spend hours seeking their staff's opinions to reassure themselves

- They delegate their duties to others but do not empower
- Delegation and empowerment are not synonymous

Another path which is less traveled because it involves risks and creates the need for the leader to stretch themself beyond their comfort zone and that is the path of the 'orangutan arms' leader.

"A state in which an individual's arms are open wide to encompass the whole situation. With your arms open wide, your mind will follow."

- They take time to self-evaluate their part in the failed situation and start again
- They listen and seek wisdom
- They reach into their pockets of experience and give it all away
- They provide the appropriate tools needed to maneuver
- They teach the way to go
- They encourage with notes, hope, smiles and positive words
- They let their associates shine

There are many avenues to take... these are only two... the choice is in your hands!

True
Leaders
have
your
back
without
recognition.

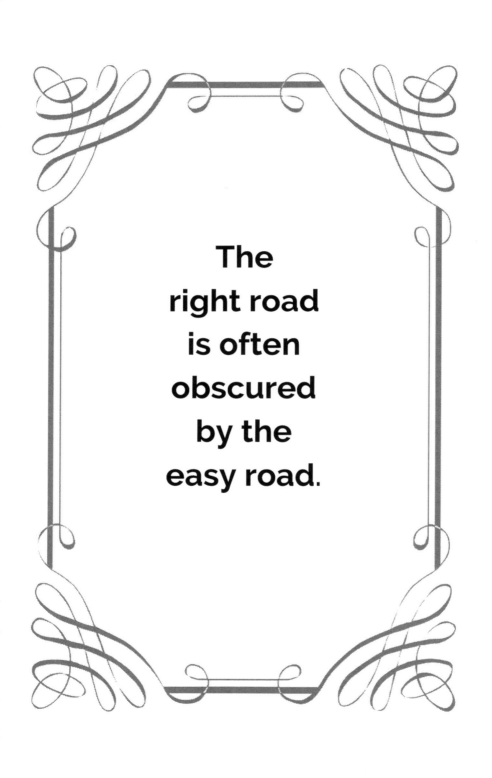

The
right road
is often
obscured
by the
easy road.

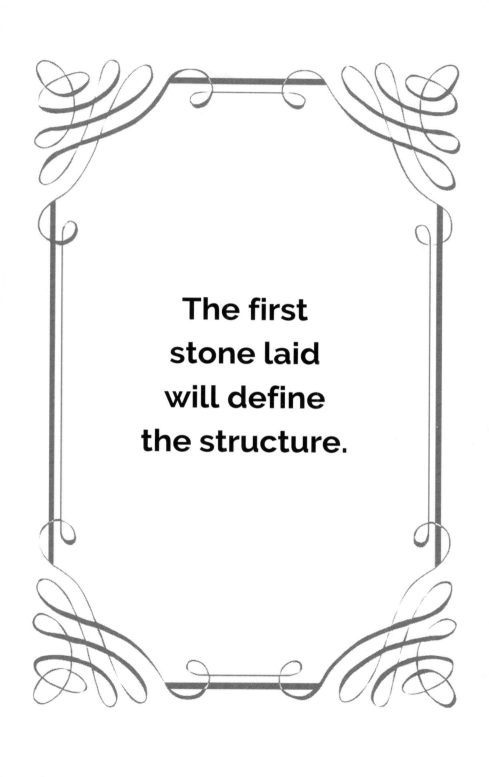

The first
stone laid
will define
the structure.

Attitudes
require
cultivation
to
grow
positive!

If you are
always busy
taking care of

#1,

you may
find yourself
stepping in

#2.

A tree
planted
in the
dessert,
will not
become
an oak!

The less you do, the less you will <u>want</u> to do!

**To find
the truth,
look behind
the veil.**

Jumping out
of an airplane
and then
building
the parachute
may not be
a good idea...

Getting people to follow you does not necessarily mean you are a good leader. Hitler had a lot of followers!

Let your
moral compass
point you to
the direction
of your future!

Ask
questions
so the
associate
can find
their own
answers.

Listen,
apply,
listen again,
re-apply,
and then
share!

Because someone is quiet in a conversation, does not mean they are listening.

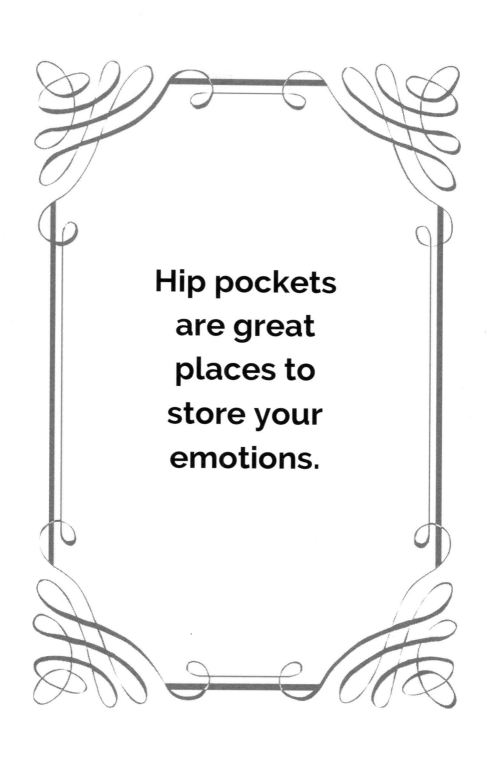

Hip pockets
are great
places to
store your
emotions.

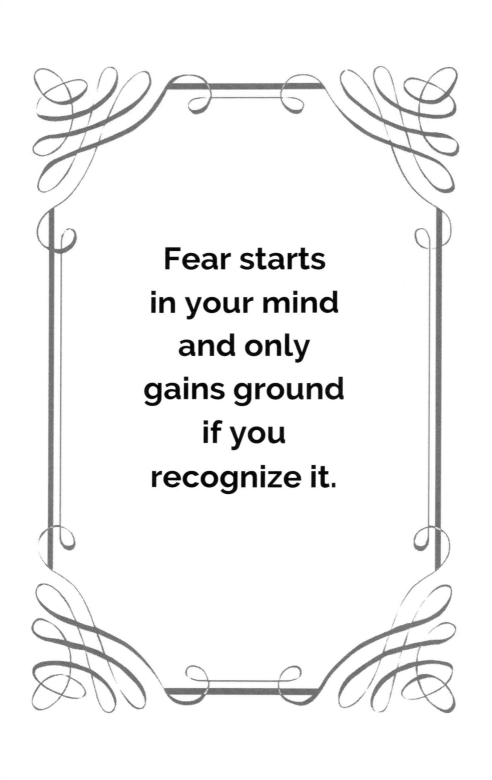

Fear starts
in your mind
and only
gains ground
if you
recognize it.

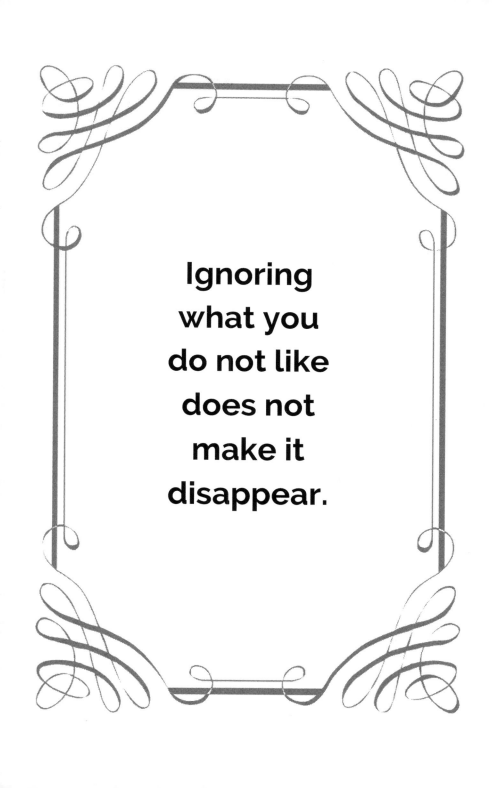

Ignoring
what you
do not like
does not
make it
disappear.

Trust and
transparency
do not run
in the same
circles as a
micromanager.

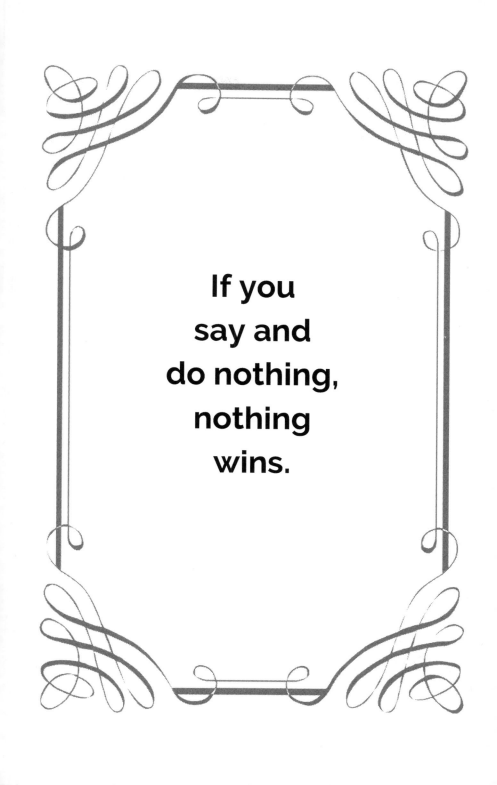

**If you
say and
do nothing,
nothing
wins.**

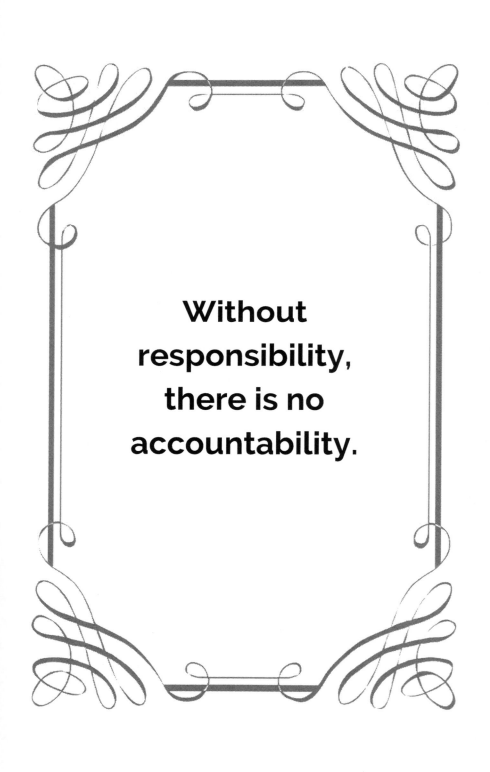

Without responsibility, there is no accountability.

There is no
accomplishment
too small
to be
recognized.

False
platitudes
are like
ships
without
rudders!

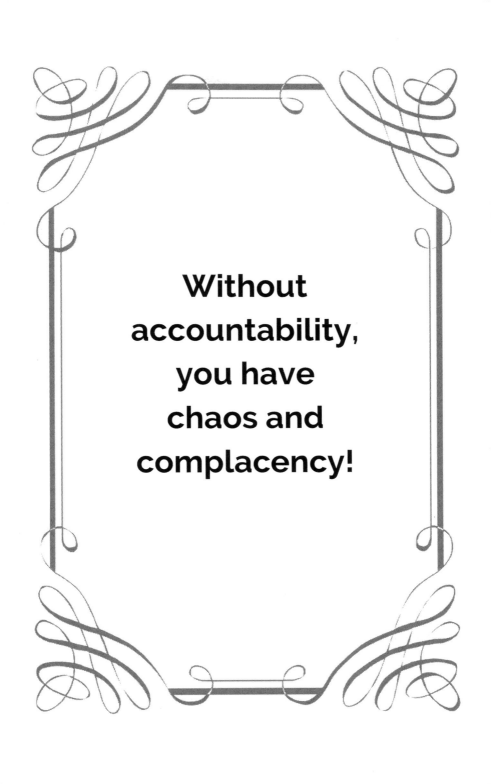

Without
accountability,
you have
chaos and
complacency!

Closed
doors
cause
silos.

5 Tips on How to Attain Influence as a Leader.

Do you have influence with your associates?

Or are they following you because you sign their paychecks?

"Leaders without influence are like leaders without followers; they are accomplishing nothing."
- John Maxwell

To keep staff motivated a leader needs to use their influence to convince them that the organization for which they work is real and is ethical enough for them to buy-in!

The 5 tips:

1. Care about the associates you work with. You have probably heard what I am about to share many times and will probably hear it again in the future. But the fact is, "staff will not care until they know you care."

2. Interact with your associates, Find out the different reasons they are there and work with them to attain their goals and fulfill their needs.

3. Be honest and communicate clearly and often. If you do not communicate well, associates will start to communicate among themselves, in what they call the 'underground network'! Without clear communications staff will start to fear that their jobs are threatened.

4. Stand up for your associates and acknowledge their successes in front of the team, in front of families and corporate. Create an environment of mutual respect, where individuality, initiative and fresh ideas are welcomed. Take action against team members who are sabotaging the efforts of the whole.

5. Set achievable goals both short term and long term. Staying excited requires frequent tastes of victory.

"If your actions inspire others to dream more, do more and become more, you are a leader."
- John Quincy Adams

The best
leadership
style
is the
one the
associate
needs.

Quality cannot be achieved without caring!

Take time
to daydream,
it refreshes
the spirit!

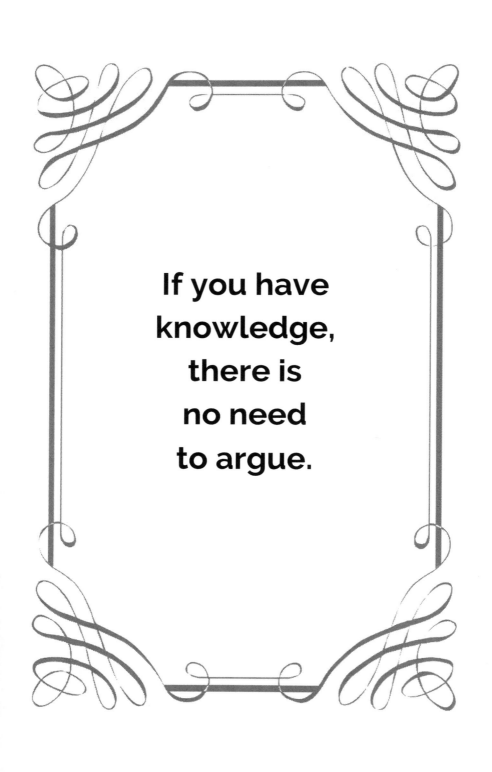

If you have
knowledge,
there is
no need
to argue.

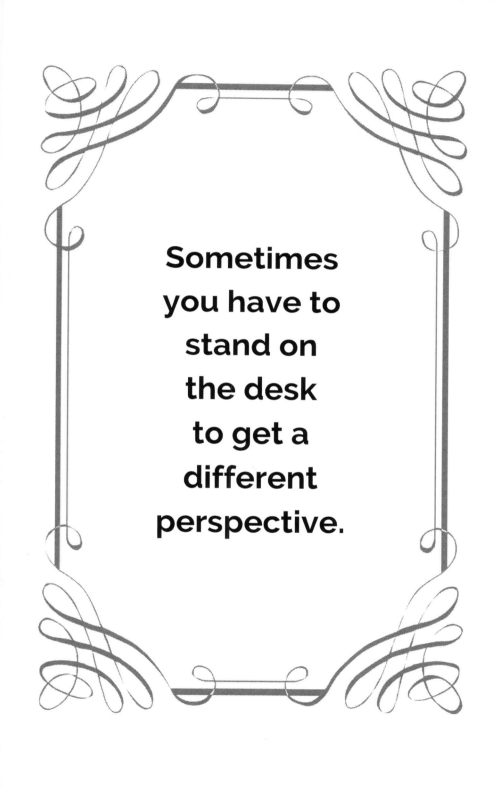

Sometimes
you have to
stand on
the desk
to get a
different
perspective.

No one style
of shoes
is right for all,
but all
need shoes!

Asking
for help
is a sign
of humility.

Organize your day and reduce impulsive actions!

Those
who lead
with a
heavy hand
break spirits.

There will
always be those
who think they
know better...

They don't!

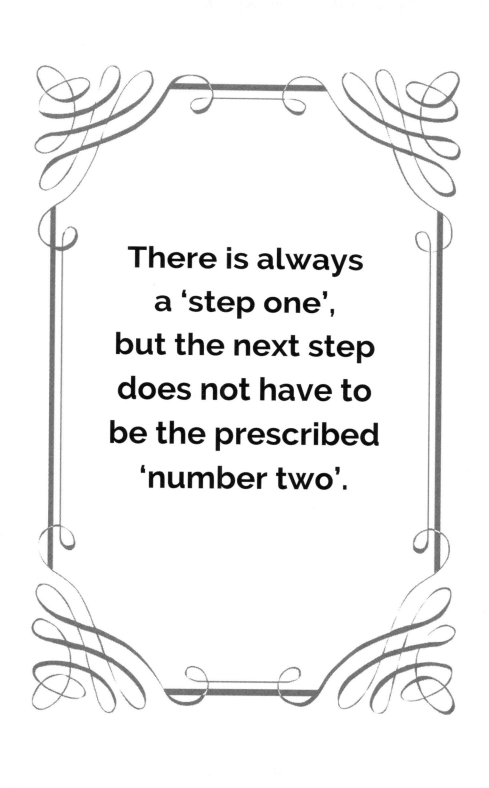

There is always
a 'step one',
but the next step
does not have to
be the prescribed
'number two'.

Stand in truth,
it is the most
fertile ground
to grow in!

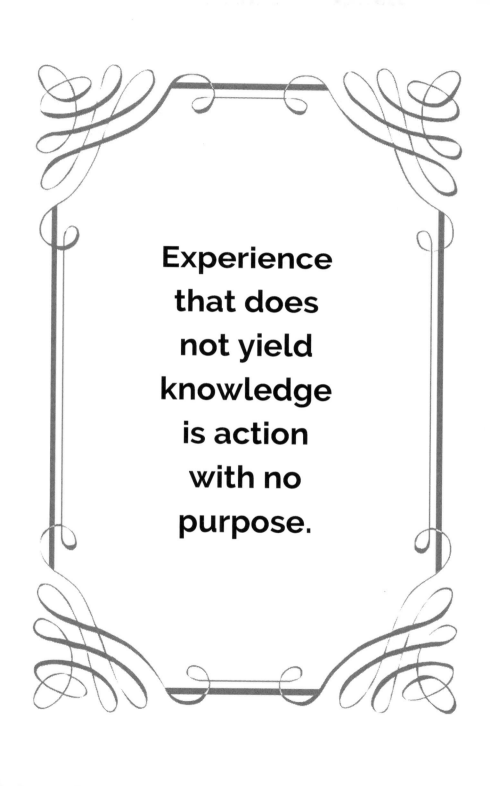

Experience
that does
not yield
knowledge
is action
with no
purpose.

Walk beside me
and you will
better understand
what I see!

Ears hear
and eyes see...

Which one
reveals more?

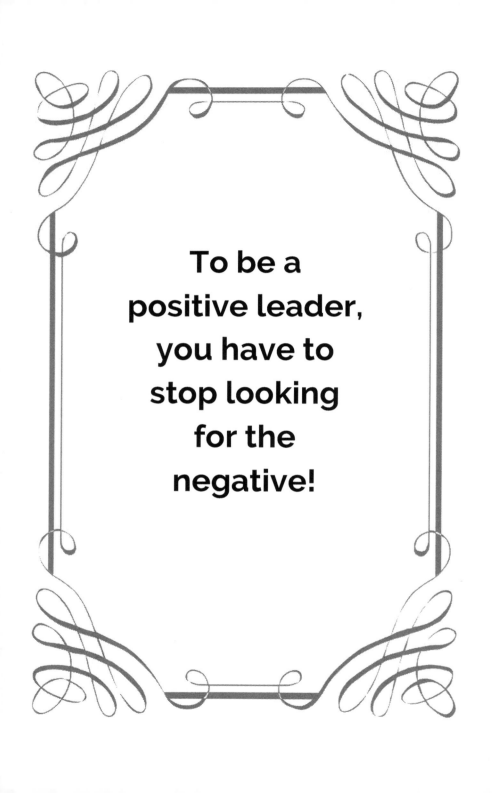

To be a positive leader, you have to stop looking for the negative!

Don't dictate
or fixate...

Communicate
and appreciate!

There is
strength
in numbers,
but it starts
with one
good leader.

The best
hand to hold
is the one
leading you
forward.

Providing
all the
answers
results in
one view!

Leadership
starts in the
mind...

Not in the
mouth!

**Never
let the
environment
dictate
your
thoughts.**

Disappointment
can not dwell
in a heart
full of
confidence!

Life is a game
of chance...

Do not be
afraid to
gamble!

Made in the USA
Columbia, SC
16 January 2021

30077488R00061